POWER
PROMISES
and
Prayers

Celebrating God's Assurances

POWER

PROMISES

and *Prayers*

Celebrating God's Assurances

Christian Book
Distributors

Christian Book
Distributors

ISBN 1-58334-142-0

The quoted ideas expressed in this book (but not scripture verses) are not, in all cases, exact quotations, as some have been edited for clarity and brevity. In all cases, the author has attempted to maintain the speaker's original intent. In some cases, quoted material for this book was obtained from secondary sources, primarily print media. While every effort was made to ensure the accuracy of these sources, the accuracy cannot be guaranteed. For additions, deletions, corrections or clarifications in future editions of this text, please write CHRISTIAN BOOK DISTRIBUTORS.

Certain elements of this text, including quotations, stories, and selected groupings of Bible verses, have appeared, in part or in whole, in publications produced by Brighton Books of Nashville, TN; these excerpts are used with permission.

Printed in the United States of America
Cover Design & Page Layout: Bart Dawson
Cover Photo: www.comstock.com

1 2 3 4 5 6 7 8 9 10 • 02 03 04 05 06 07 08 09 10

Dedicated to Those Who Trust
in the Word of God

TABLE OF CONTENTS

TABLE OF CONTENTS

TABLE OF CONTENTS

Introduction

God's power is beyond human comprehension, but His promises are not. While we, as mere human beings, can never fully understand our Creator, we can understand His Word, and we can choose to follow it...or not. When we align our lives with God's will, when we live by the commandments of His Holy Word, we are the beneficiaries of His power and His grace. But, if we stray from His commandments, we bring untold suffering into our own lives and the lives of those we love.

This text is intended to help readers understand and claim the powerful, life-changing promises that God has made to His Children. The power of prayer in the lives of righteous men and women of every generation bears testimony to the dependence of mankind on a benevolent, caring God. You, too, can claim God's promises; all you must do is to seek His grace and follow His commandments.

Every morning, the dawn breaks upon a world filled with countless opportunities to serve God and to praise Him. Many days bring excitement and celebration while other days bring disappointment or sadness. Whatever the day brings—whether joy or despair—God remains steadfast, ready to protect you and empower you...if you let Him.

This book addresses topics of profound importance to Christians. Each chapter contains Bible verses, a brief word of encouragement, a quotation, and a prayer. As you begin each day, or as you face challenges that may occur during your day, consult these pages. When you do, you will be reminded that an all-powerful God has made important promises to you, promises for today and promises for all of eternity. And rest assured: God always keeps his promises. Always.

Abundance

...my cup runneth over. Surely goodness and mercy shall follow me all the days of my life: and I will dwell in the house of the LORD for ever.

Psalm 23:5,6 KJV

...I am come that they might have life, and that they might have it more abundantly.

John 10:10 KJV

But this I say, He which soweth sparingly shall reap also sparingly; and he which soweth bountifully shall reap also bountifully.

2 Corinthians 9:6 KJV

His master replied, "Well done, good and faithful servant! You have been faithful with a few things; I will put you in charge of many things. Come and share your master's happiness!"

Matthew 25:21

The 10th chapter of John tells us that Christ came to earth so that our lives might be filled with abundance. But what, exactly, did Jesus mean when He promised "life...more abundantly"? Was Jesus referring to material possessions or financial wealth? Hardly. He offered a different kind of abundance: a spiritual richness that extends beyond the temporal boundaries of this world. This everlasting abundance is available to all who seek it and claim it. May we, as believers, claim the riches of Christ Jesus every day that we live, and may we share His riches with all who cross our path.

People, places, and things were never meant to give us life. God alone is the author of a fulfilling life.

Gary Smalley & John Trent

Heavenly Father, You have promised an abundant life through Your Son Jesus. Thank You, Lord, for Your abundance. Guide me according to Your will, so that I might be a worthy servant in all that I say and do, this day and every day.

Amen

Accepting Christ

For God so loved the world, that he gave his only begotten Son, that whosoever believeth in him should not perish, but have everlasting life.

John 3:16 KJV

For there is one God and one mediator between God and men, the man Christ Jesus, who gave himself as a ransom for all men....

1 Timothy 2:5,6

Jesus answered, "I am the way and the truth and the life. No one comes to the Father except through me."

John 14:6

That if thou shalt confess with thy mouth the Lord Jesus, and shalt believe in thine heart that God hath raised him from the dead, thou shalt be saved. For with the heart man believeth unto righteousness; and with the mouth confession is made unto salvation.

Romans 10:9,10 KJV

God loves you. Period. His affection for you is deeper and more profound than you can imagine. God's love for you is so great that He sent His only Son to this earth to die for your sins and offer you the priceless gift of eternal life. Now, you must decide whether or not to accept God's gift. Will you ignore it or embrace it? Will you return it or neglect it? Will you accept Christ or not? The decision, of course, is yours and yours alone, and the decision has eternal consequences. Accept God's gift: Accept Christ.

Our salvation comes to us so easily because it cost God so much.

Oswald Chambers

Dear Lord, when You invited me to be part of Your family, I said yes. I confessed that Jesus was my Lord and Savior, and You saved me. I choose, this day, to live in such a way that others might also accept Christ as their Savior and that they might see my love for You reflected through my words and my deeds.

Amen

Adversity

...Be strong and courageous. Do not be terrified; do not be discouraged, for the Lord your God will be with you wherever you go.

Joshua 1:9-10

Then they cried unto the LORD in their trouble, and he saved them out of their distresses.

Psalm 107:13 KJV

For whatsoever is born of God overcometh the world....

1 John 5:4 KJV

When you go through deep waters and great trouble, I will be with you. When you go through the rivers of difficulty, you will not drown! When you walk through the fire of oppression, you will not be burned up; the flames will not consume you. For I am the Lord, your God....

Isaiah 43:2-3 NLT

All of us face adversity, discouragement, or disappointment. When we do, God stands ready to protect us. Psalm 147 promises believers that He heals the brokenhearted and binds their wounds (v. 3). When we are troubled, we must call upon God, and then, in His own time and according to His own plan, He will heal us.

When God is going to do a wonderful thing, He begins with a difficulty. When He is going to do a very wonderful thing, he begins with an impossibility.

Charles Inwood

Dear Heavenly Father, when I am troubled, You heal me. When I am afraid, You protect me. When I am discouraged, You lift me up. You are my unending source of strength, Lord; let me turn to You when I am weak. In times of adversity, let me trust Your plan and Your will for my life. And whatever my circumstances, Lord, let me always give the thanks and the glory to You.

Amen

Anger

Wise men turn away anger.

Proverbs 29:8 NASB

You have heard it said, 'Love your neighbor and hate your enemy' But I tell you: Love your enemies and pray for those who persecute you, that you may be sons of your father in heaven.

Matthew 5:43-45

Let all bitterness, and wrath, and anger, and clamor, and evil speaking, be put away from you, with all malice: and be ye kind one to another, tender-hearted, forgiving one another, even as God for Christ's sake hath forgiven you.

Ephesians 4:31-32 KJV

...do not let the sun go down on your anger, and do not give the devil an opportunity.

Ephesians 4:26-27 NASB

Anger is a natural human emotion that is sometimes necessary and appropriate. Jesus Himself became angered when He confronted the money-changers in the temple. But, more often than not, our frustrations are of the more mundane variety. When you are tempted to lose your temper over the minor inconveniences of life, don't. Turn away from anger, and turn instead to God.

Anger: the noise of the soul; the unseen irritant of the heart; the relentless invader of silence.... The past cannot change, but your response to your past can.

Max Lucado

Lord, sometimes, I am quick to anger and slow to forgive. But I know, Lord, that You seek abundance and peace for my life. Forgiveness is Your commandment; empower me to follow the example of Your Son Jesus who forgave His persecutors. As I turn away from anger, I claim the peace that You intend for my life.

Amen

Asking God

Ask and it will be given you; seek and you will find; knock and the door will be opened to you. For everyone who asks receives; he who seeks finds; and to him who knocks, the door is opened.

Matthew 7:7-8

Verily, verily, I say unto you, He that believeth on me, the works that I do shall he do also; and greater works than these shall he do; because I go unto my Father. And whatsoever ye shall ask in my name, that will I do, that the Father may be glorified in the Son. If ye shall ask any thing in my name, I will do it.

John 14:12-14 KJV

...You do not have because you do not ask God.

James 4:2

Are you in need? Ask God to sustain you. Are you troubled? Take your worries to Him in prayer. Are you weary? Seek God's strength. In all things great and small, seek the healing power of God's grace. He hears your prayers, and He will answer.

Some people think God does not like to be troubled with our constant asking. The way to trouble God is not to come at all.

D. L. Moody

Lord...You are the giver of all things good. When I am in need, I come to You in prayer. You know the desires of my heart, Lord. Grant them, I ask, yet not my will but Your will be done.

Amen

Attitude

You were taught, with regard to your former way of life, to put off your old self, which is being corrupted by its deceitful desires; to be made new in the attitude of your minds; and to put on the new self, created to be like God in true righteousness and holiness.

Ephesians 4:22-24

Set your mind on the things above, not on the things that are on earth.

Colossians 3:2 NASB

Your attitude should be the same as that of Christ Jesus: Who, being in very nature God, did not consider equality with God something to be grasped, but made himself nothing, taking the very nature of a servant, being made in human likeness. And being found in appearance as a man, he humbled himself and became obedient to death— even death on a cross!

Philippians 2:5-8

As Christians, we have every reason to rejoice. God's promises are unambiguous: He is in His heaven; Christ has risen, and we are the sheep of His flock. Today, we stand on the certainty of those promises as we count our blessings instead of our hardships. And, we thank an all-powerful God for gifts that are simply too numerous to count.

Attitude is all-important. Let the soul take a quiet attitude of faith and love toward God, and from there on the responsibility is God's. He will make good on His commitments.

A. W. Tozer

Lord...I pray for an attitude that is Christlike as I trust completely in the promises of Your Holy Word. And whatever circumstances I face, whether good or bad, triumphal or tragic, empower me to reflect a God-honoring, Christlike attitude of optimism, faith, and love for You...today, tomorrow, and forever.

Amen

Behavior

I the Lord search the heart and examine the mind, to reward a man according to his conduct, according to what his deeds deserve.

Jeremiah 17:10

Who among you is wise and understanding? Let him show by his good behavior his deeds in the gentleness of wisdom.

James 3:13 NASB

If we live in the Spirit, let us also walk in the Spirit.

Galatians 5:25 KJV

And you shall do what is good and right in the sight of the Lord, that it may be well with you....

Deuteronomy 6:18 NASB

Decisions, decisions, decisions... We have so many decisions each day and so many opportunities to stray from God's commandments. When we live according to God's commandments and follow His will, we earn for ourselves the abundance and peace that God will provide for our lives. May we, as believers in Christ, claim God's power and His peace by worshiping Him and obeying Him.

Be such a man, and live such a life, that if every man were such as you, and every life a life like yours, this earth would be God's Paradise.

Phillips Brooks

Lord, it is so much easier to speak of the righteous life than it is to live it. Enable me to live righteously, and let my actions be consistent with my beliefs. Make every step that I take reflect Your truth and Your love, and may I live a life that is worthy of Your love and Your grace.

Amen

The Bible

Heaven and earth will pass away, but my words will never pass away.

Matthew 24:35

If ye abide in me, and my words abide in you, ye shall ask what ye will, and it shall be done unto you.

John 15:7 KJV

But he answered and said, It is written, Man shall not live by bread alone, but by every word that proceedeth out of the mouth of God.

Matthew 4:4 KJV

Every word of God is flawless; he is a shield to those who take refuge in him.

Proverbs 30:5

God has given us the Holy Bible for the purpose of knowing His promises, His power, His commandments, His wisdom, His love, and His Son. As we study God's teachings and apply them to our lives, we live by the Word that shall never pass away.

If you see a Bible that is falling apart, it probably belongs to someone who isn't.

Vance Havner

Dear Lord, the Bible is Your gift to me; thank You. When I stray from Your Holy Word, Lord, I suffer. But, when I place Your Word at the very center of my life, I am protected and blessed. Make me a faithful student of Your Word.

Amen

Celebration

Rejoice, and be exceeding glad: for great is your reward in heaven....

Matthew 5:12 KJV

Shout for joy to the LORD, all the earth. Worship the LORD with gladness; come before him with joyful songs.

Psalm 100:1-2

This is the day the Lord has made; let us rejoice and be glad in it.

Psalm 118:24

...let the hearts of those who seek the Lord rejoice. Look to the Lord and his strength; seek his face always.

1 Chronicles 16:10-11

The 118th Psalm reminds us that today, like every other day, is a cause for celebration. God gives us this day; He fills it to the brim with possibilities, and He challenges us to use it for His purposes. The day is presented to us fresh and clean at midnight, free of charge, but we must beware: Today is a non-renewable resource—once it's gone, it's gone forever. Our responsibility, of course, is to use this day in the service of God's will and according to His commandments.

A child of God should be a visible beatitude for joy and happiness, and a living doxology for gratitude and adoration.

C. H. Spurgeon

Lord God, You have created a grand and glorious universe that is far beyond human understanding. The heavens proclaim Your handiwork, and every star in the sky tells of Your power. Let me celebrate You and Your marvelous creation, Lord, and let me rejoice in this day and every day, now and forever. Today is Your gift to me, Lord. Let me use it to Your glory while giving all the praise to You.

Amen

Character

May integrity and uprightness protect me, because my hope is in you.

Psalm 25:21

...in all things showing yourself to be a pattern of good works; in doctrine showing integrity, reverence, incorruptibility....

Titus 2:7 NKJV

As in water face reflects face, so the heart of man reflects man.

Proverbs 27:19 NASB

A good name is rather to be chosen than great riches....

Proverbs 22:1 KJV

Character is built slowly over a lifetime. It is the sum of every right decision, every honest word, every noble thought, and every heartfelt prayer. It is forged on the anvil of honorable work and polished by the twin virtues of generosity and humility. Character is a precious thing—difficult to build but easy to tear down. As believers in Christ, we must seek to live each day with discipline, honesty, and faith. When we do, integrity becomes a habit. And God smiles.

There is no way to grow a saint overnight. Character, like the oak tree, does not spring up like a mushroom.

Vance Havner

Lord...You are my Father in Heaven. You search my heart and know me far better than I know myself. Today, I choose to be Your servant and to live according to Your commandments. Empower me to be a person of integrity, Lord, and let my words and deeds be a testimony to You.

Amen

Cheerfulness

...the cheerful heart has a continual feast.

Proverbs 15:15

A cheerful heart is good medicine....

Proverbs 17:22

You will show me the path of life; In Your presence *is* fullness of joy; At Your right hand there *are* pleasures forevermore.

Psalm 16:11 NKJV

Shout for joy to the LORD, all the earth, burst into jubilant song with music; make music to the LORD with the harp, with the harp and the sound of singing, with trumpets and the blast of the ram's horn—shout for joy before the LORD, the King.

Psalm 98:4-6

Few things in life are more sad, or, for that matter, more absurd, than a grumpy Christian. Christ promises us a life of abundance and joy, but He does not force His joy upon us. We must claim His joy for ourselves, and when we do, Jesus, in turn, fills our spirits with His power and His love. Then we, as God's children, can share Christ's joy and His message with a world that needs both.

When I think of God, my heart is so full of joy that the notes leap and dance as they leave my pen; and since God has given me a cheerful heart, I serve him with a cheerful spirit.

Franz Joseph Haydn

Dear Lord, You have given me so many reasons to celebrate. Today, I choose an attitude of cheerfulness. Let me be a joyful Christian, Lord, quick to smile and slow to anger. And, I will share Your goodness with all whom I meet so that Your love might shine in me and through me.

Amen

Christ's Love

For I am persuaded, that neither death, nor life, nor angels, nor principalities, nor powers, nor things present, nor things to come, nor height, nor depth, nor any other creature, shall be able to separate us from the love of God, which is in Christ Jesus our Lord.

Romans 8:38-39 KJV

As the Father hath loved me, so have I loved you; continue ye in my love.

John 15:9 KJV

God is love; and he that dwelleth in love dwelleth in God, and God in him.

1 John 4:16 KJV

We love him, because he first loved us.

1 John 4:19 KJV

Although we are imperfect, fallible human beings, and even though we have fallen far short of God's commandments, Christ loves us still. His love is perfect and steadfast; it does not waver. As we accept Christ's love and live in Christ's love, our lives bear testimony to His power and to His grace. Christ's love changes everything; may we, as believers, accept it and share it.

For nourishment, comfort, exhilaration, and refreshment, no wine can rival the love of Jesus. Drink deeply.

C. H. Spurgeon

Dear Jesus...I am humbled by Your love and mercy. You went to Calvary so that I might have eternal life. Thank You, Jesus, for Your priceless gift, and for Your love. You loved me first, Lord, and I will return Your love today and forever.

Amen

Conscience

So I strive always to keep my conscience clear before God and man.

Acts 24:16

...let us draw near to God with a sincere heart in full assurance of faith, having our hearts sprinkled to cleanse us from a guilty conscience and having our bodies washed with pure water.

Hebrews 10:22

Do not conform any longer to the pattern of this world, but be transformed by the renewing of your mind. Then you will be able to test and approve what God's will is—his good, pleasing and perfect will.

Romans 12:2

Since, then, you have been raised with Christ, set your hearts on things above, where Christ is seated at the right hand of God. Set your minds on things above, not on earthly things.

Colossians 3:1,2

Few things in life torment us more than a guilty conscience. And, few things in life provide more contentment than the knowledge that we are obeying God's commandments. A clear conscience is one of the rewards we earn when we obey God's Word and follow His will. As we follow God's will and accept His gift of salvation, our earthly rewards are never-ceasing, and our heavenly rewards are everlasting.

There is no pillow so soft as a clear conscience.

French Proverb

Lord...You speak to me through the Bible, through teachers, and through friends. And, Father, You speak to me through that still, small voice that warns me when I stray from Your will. In these quiet moments and throughout the day, show me Your plan for my life, Lord, that I might serve You.

Amen

Contentment

But godliness with contentment is great gain. For we brought nothing into the world, and we can take nothing out of it. But if we have food and clothing, we will be content with that.

1 Timothy 6:6-8

Let your conduct be without covetousness; be content with such things as you have. For He Himself has said, "I will never leave you nor forsake you."

Hebrews 13:5 NKJV

Because your love is better than life, my lips will glorify you. I will praise you as long as I live, and in your name I will lift up my hands. My soul will be satisfied as with the richest of foods; with singing lips my mouth will praise you.

Psalm 63:3-5

Where can we find contentment? Is it a result of wealth, or power, or fame? Hardly. Genuine contentment is a gift from God to those who trust in Him and follow His commandments. When God dwells at the center of our families and our lives, contentment will belong to us just as surely as we belong to God.

Make God's will as the focus of your life day by day. If you seek to please Him and Him alone, you'll find yourself satisfied with life.

Kay Arthur

Father...You are my contentment. Whatever my circumstances, I find contentment when I seek Your healing hand. I look to You, Father, for the power and the peace that You have offered me through the gift of Your Son. Let me accept Your precious gift, and let me share it.

Amen

Courage

...Be strong and courageous, and do the work. Do not be afraid or discouraged, for the Lord God, my God, is with you.

1 Chronicles 28:20

The Lord is my light and my salvation; whom shall I fear? The Lord is the strength of my life; of whom shall I be afraid?

Psalm 27:1 KJV

I sought the LORD, and he heard me, and delivered me from all my fears.

Psalm 34:4 KJV

And the Lord appeared to him...and said, Fear not, for I am with you, and will bless you.

Genesis 26:24 NKJV

When the storm clouds form overhead and we find ourselves in the dark valley of despair, our faith is stretched, sometimes to the breaking point. As Christians, we can be comforted: Wherever we find ourselves, whether at the top of the mountain or the depths of the valley, God is there. And, because He cares for us, we can live courageously.

Down through the centuries, in times of trouble and trial, God has brought courage to the hearts of those who love Him. The Bible is filled with assurances of God's help and comfort in every kind of trouble which might cause fears to arise in the human heart. You can look ahead with promise, hope, and joy.

Billy Graham

Lord...sometimes, this world can be a fearful place. Yet, You have promised me that You are with me always. With You as my protector, I am not afraid. Today, Dear Lord, I will live courageously as I place my trust in Your everlasting power and my faith in Your everlasting love.

Amen

Diligence

And we desire that each one of you show the same diligence so as to realize the full assurance of hope until the end, so that you will not be sluggish, but imitators of those who through faith and patience inherit the promises.

Hebrews 6:11-12 NASB

He who tills his land will have plenty of food, but he who follows empty pursuits will have poverty in plenty.

Proverbs 28:19 NASB

He did it with all his heart, and prospered.

2 Chronicles 31:21 KJV

Whatever you do, work at it with all your heart, as working for the Lord, not for men.

Colossians 3:23

As we study the Bible, we are confronted again and again with God's intention that we, as believers in Christ, lead disciplined lives. God does not reward laziness nor does he praise mediocrity. To the contrary, He expects us to be disciplined, diligent, and faithful to His commandments. As we begin this day, let us remember that God rewards diligence. And let us act accordingly.

If God is diligent, surely we ought to be diligent in doing our duty to Him. Think how patient and diligent God has been to us!

Oswald Chambers

Lord, You have given me this day that I might do Your will. Let me do so with courage and commitment. The work I have before me today is really Your work. Help me to use my talents to the best of my ability. And may the glory from my efforts be Your glory, this day and forever.

Amen

Encouraging Others

A cheerful look brings joy to the heart, and good news gives health to the bones.

Proverbs 15:30

Let us consider how to stimulate one another to love and good deeds.

Hebrews 10:24 NASB

We urge you, brethren, admonish the unruly, encourage the fainthearted, help the weak, be patient with all men.

1 Thessalonians 5:14 NASB

Let the word of Christ dwell in you richly in all wisdom; teaching and admonishing one another in psalms and hymns and spiritual songs, singing with grace in your hearts to the Lord.

Colossians 3:16 KJV

The 118th Psalm reminds us, "This is the day which the Lord hath made; we will rejoice and be glad in it" (v. 24 KJV). Let us remember that an important part of today's celebration is the time we spend celebrating others. Each day provides countless opportunities to encourage others and to praise their good works. Our families and friends need honest, heartfelt encouragement. We all do. And, when we lift each other up, we follow the will and the Word of God.

There are no words to express the abyss between isolation and having one ally. It may be conceded to the mathematician that four is twice two. But two is not twice one; two is two thousand times one.

G. K. Chesterton

Make me sensitive, O Lord, to the many gifts of encouragement I receive each day. And, let me be a source of encouragement to all who cross my path. The Bible tells of Your servant Barnabas. Like Barnabas, I, too, want to be an encourager to my family and friends so that I might do Your work and share Your love.

Amen

Eternal Life

For God so loved the world, that he gave his only begotten Son, that whosoever believeth in him should not perish, but have everlasting life.

John 3:16 KJV

Verily, verily, I say unto you, He that heareth my word, and believeth on him that sent me, hath everlasting life, and shall not come into condemnation; but is passed from death unto life.

John 5:24 KJV

For the wages of sin is death, but the gift of God is eternal life in Christ Jesus our Lord.

Romans 6:23

And this is the will of him that sent me, that every one which seeth the Son, and believeth on him, may have everlasting life: and I will raise him up at the last day.

John 6:40 KJV

Christ sacrificed His life on the cross so that we might have eternal life. This gift, freely given from God's only begotten Son, is the priceless possession of everyone who accepts Him as Lord and savior. God is waiting patiently for each of us to accept the gift of eternal life. Let us claim Christ's gift today.

Teach us to set our hopes on heaven, to hold firmly to the promise of eternal life, so that we can withstand the struggles and storms of this world.

Max Lucado

Lord, I am only here on this earth for a brief while. But, You have offered me the priceless gift of eternal life through Your Son Jesus. I accept Your gift, Lord, with thanksgiving and praise. Today and every day, let me share the good news of my salvation with those who need Your healing touch.

Amen

Evil

Submit yourselves therefore to God. Resist the devil, and he will flee from you. Draw nigh to God, and he will draw nigh to you.

James 4:7-8 KJV

Be not overcome of evil, but overcome evil with good.

Romans 12:21 KJV

He shall not be afraid of evil tidings: his heart is fixed, trusting in the LORD.

Psalm 112:7 KJV

Be self-controlled and alert. Your enemy the devil prowls around like a roaring lion looking for someone to devour. Resist him, standing firm in the faith....

1 Peter 5:8,9

This world is God's creation, and it contains the wonderful fruits of His handiwork. But, it also contains countless opportunities to stray from God's will. Temptations are everywhere, and the devil, it seems, never takes a day off. Our task, as believers, is to turn away from temptation and to place our lives squarely in the center of God's will. As we do, evil can never conquer us because we are protected by an all-powerful and all-loving God.

The only thing necessary for the triumph of evil is for good men to do nothing.

Edmund Burke

Strengthen my walk with You, my heavenly Father. Evil comes in so many disguises that sometimes it is only with Your help that I can recognize right from wrong. Your presence in my life enables me to choose truth and to live a life that is pleasing to You. May I always live in Your presence.

Amen

Faith

Let us hold fast the profession of our faith without wavering; for he is faithful....

Hebrews 10:23 KJV

But without faith it is impossible to please him: for he that cometh to God must believe that he is, and that he is a rewarder of them that diligently seek him.

Hebrews 11:6 KJV

Fight the good fight of faith; take hold of the eternal life to which you were called....

1 Timothy 6:12 NASB

...If ye have faith as a grain of mustard seed, ye shall say unto this mountain, Remove hence to yonder place; and it shall remove: and nothing shall be impossible unto you.

Matthew 17:20 KJV

Have you, on occasion, felt your faith in God slipping away? If so, welcome to the club. We, as mere mortals, are subject to emotions like fear, worry, and doubt. When we fall short of perfect faith, God understands us and forgives us. And, God stands ready to strengthen us, to bless us, and to renew us if we turn our doubts and fears over to Him.

Faith is a living, daring confidence in God's grace, so sure and certain that a man would stake his life on it a thousand times.

Martin Luther

Dear God, this world can be a fearful place, full of uncertainty and doubt. In those dark moments, help me to remember that You are always near and that You can overcome any challenge. Give me faith and let me remember always that with Your love and Your power, I can live courageously and faithfully today and every day.

Amen

Fear

For God hath not given us the spirit of fear; but of power, and of love, and of a sound mind.

2 Timothy 1:7 KJV

Don't be afraid, for I am with you. Do not be dismayed for I am your God. I will strengthen you. I will help you. I will uphold you with my victorious right hand.

Isaiah 41:10 NLT

...Be not afraid, only believe.

Mark 5:36 KJV

I cried out to the Lord in my suffering, and he heard me. He set me free from all my fears.

Psalm 34:6 NLT

Even dedicated followers of Christ may find their courage tested by the inevitable disappointments and tragedies of life. The next time you find your courage tested, remember that God is as near as your next breath, and remember that He offers salvation to His children. He is your shield and your strength. Call upon Him in your hour of need and be comforted. Whatever the size of your challenge, God is bigger.

Earthly fears are no fears at all. Answer the big question of eternity, and the little questions of life fall into perspective.

Max Lucado

Your Word reminds me, Lord, that even when I walk through the valley of the shadow of death, I need fear no evil, for You are with me, and You comfort me. Thank You, Lord, for a perfect love that casts out fear. Let me live courageously and faithfully this day and every day.

Amen

Fear of God

How blessed is everyone who fears the LORD, who walks in His ways.

Psalm 128:1 NASB

The fear of the Lord is the beginning of wisdom, and knowledge of the Holy One is understanding.

Proverbs 9:10

Fear the LORD your God, serve him only and take your oaths in his name.

Deuteronomy 6:13

The fear of the Lord is a fountain of life....

Proverbs 14:27

The Book of Proverbs tells us that the fear of the Lord is the beginning of knowledge. When we fear God and obey His Holy Word, we receive His love and His grace. But, when we ignore Him or disobey His commandments, we invite disastrous consequences. Today, may we honor God and respect Him by obeying His commandments.

The remarkable thing about fearing God is that when you fear God, you fear nothing else; whereas, if you do not fear God, you fear everything else.

Oswald Chambers

Dear Lord, others have expectations of me, and I have hopes and desires for my life. Lord, bring all other expectation in line with Your plans for me. May my only fear be that of displeasing the One who created me. Let me obey Your commandments and seek Your will and, in doing so, Honor the One who created me and saved me.

Amen

Forgiveness

And be ye kind one to another, tender-hearted, forgiving one another, even as God for Christ's sake hath forgiven you.

Ephesians 4:32 KJV

Whenever you stand praying, forgive, if you have anything against anyone, so that your Father in heaven will also forgive you your transgressions.

Mark 11:25 NASB

Then came Peter to him, and said, Lord, how oft shall my brother sin against me, and I forgive him? till seven times? Jesus saith unto him, I say not unto thee, Until seven times: but, Until seventy times seven.

Matthew 18:21-22 KJV

Blessed are the merciful: for they shall obtain mercy.

Matthew 5:7 KJV

We are frail, fallible, imperfect human beings, and, thus, we are quick to anger, quick to blame, slow to forgive, and even slower to forget. But, forgiveness is God's way, and it must be our way, too. If there exists even one person, alive or dead, whom you have not forgiven (and that includes yourself), follow God's commandment and His will for your life: forgive. Hatred and bitterness and regret are not part of God's plan for your life. Forgiveness is.

Jesus had a forgiving and understanding heart. If he lives within us, mercy will temper our relationships with our fellow men.

Billy Graham

Heavenly Father, forgiveness is Your commandment, and I know that I need to forgive others just as You have forgiven me. But, genuine forgiveness is difficult. Empower me to forgive those who have injured me, and deliver me from the traps of anger and bitterness. Forgiveness is Your way, Lord; make it mine.

Amen

Generosity

Let us not lose heart in doing good, for in due time we will reap if we do not grow weary. So then, while we have opportunity, let us do good to all people, and especially to those who are of the household of the faith.

Galatians 6:9-10 NASB

... so let him give; not grudgingly, or of necessity: for God loveth a cheerful giver.

2 Corinthians 9:7 KJV

Freely you have received, freely give.

Matthew 10:8

It is well with the man who deals generously and lends.

Psalm 112:5 RSV

As believers, we are blessed here on earth, and we are blessed eternally through God's grace. We can never fully repay God for His gifts, but we can share them with others. We do so by showing kindness and generosity to those who enter our lives.

We are never more like God than when we give to others.

Chuck Swindoll

Father...Your gifts are beyond comprehension. You gave Your Son Jesus to save us, and Your motivation was love. I pray that the gifts I give to others will come from an overflow of my heart, and that they will echo the great love You have for all of Your children.

Amen

Gifts

Do not neglect the spiritual gift that is within you....

1 Timothy 4:14 NASB

Every good gift and every perfect gift is from above, and cometh down from the Father of lights.

James 1:17 KJV

Since we have gifts that differ according to the grace given to us, each of us is to exercise them accordingly: if prophecy, according to the proportion of his faith; if service, in his serving; or he who teaches, in his teaching; or he who exhorts, in his exhortation; he who gives, with liberality; he who leads, with diligence; he who shows mercy, with cheerfulness.

Romans 12:6-8 NASB

All of us have special gifts, and you are no exception. But, your gift is no guarantee of success; it must be cultivated and nurtured; otherwise, it will go unused…and God's gift to you will be squandered. Today, accept this challenge: value the gift that God has given you, nourish it, make it grow, and share it with the world. After all, the best way to say "Thank You" for God's gifts is to use them.

In the great orchestra we call life, you have an instrument and a song, and you owe it to God to play them both sublimely.

Max Lucado

You have gifted me with abilities to be used for You, dear Lord. Help me not to focus on how much or how little talent I have, but instead to focus on using, to the fullest, the gifts You have given me.

Amen

God's Blessings

For thou, LORD, wilt bless the righteous....

Psalm 5:12 KJV

I will bless them and the places surrounding my hill. I will send down showers in season; there will be showers of blessings.

Ezekial 34:26

Blessings crown the head of the righteous....

Proverbs 10:6

God gives us blessings that are too numerous to count. Your blessings include life, family, freedom, friends, talents, and possessions, for starters. But, your greatest blessing—a gift that is yours for the asking—is God's gift of salvation through Christ Jesus. Today, give thanks for your blessings and show your thanks by using them and by sharing them.

Jesus intended for us to be overwhelmed by the blessings of regular days. He said it was the reason he had come: "I am come that they might have life, and that they might have it more abundantly" (John 10:10 KJV).

Gloria Gaither

Today, Lord, let me count my blessings with thanksgiving in my heart. You have cared for me, Lord, and I will give You the glory and the praise. Let me accept Your blessings and Your gifts, and let me share them with others, just as You first shared them with me.

Amen

God's Commandments

For this is the love of God, that we keep his commandments....

1 John 5:3 KJV

He that hath my commandments, and keepeth them, he it is that loveth me: and he that loveth me shall be loved of my Father, and I will love him, and will manifest myself to him.

John 14:21 KJV

Whoso despiseth the word shall be destroyed: but he that feareth the commandment shall be rewarded.

Proverbs 13:13 KJV

Happy are those who fear the Lord. Yes, happy are those who delight in doing his commands.

Psalm 112:1 NLT

God has given us a guidebook for righteous living called the Holy Bible. It contains thorough instructions which, when followed, lead to fulfillment, righteousness, and salvation. But, if we choose to ignore God's commandments, the results are as predictable as they are tragic. Let us follow God's commandments, and let us conduct our lives in such a way that we might be shining examples for those who have not yet found Christ.

If men will not be governed by the Ten Commandments they shall be governed by the ten thousand commandments.

G. K. Chesterton

Thank You, Dear Lord, for loving me enough to give me rules to live by. As I live by Your commandments, let me lead others to do the same. Give me the wisdom to walk righteously in Your way, Dear Lord, trusting always in You.

Amen

God's Grace

But by the grace of God I am what I am, and his grace to me was not without effect. No, I worked harder than all of them—yet not I, but the grace of God that was with me.

1 Corinthians 15:10

For by grace you have been saved through faith, and that not of yourselves; it is the gift of God, not of works, lest anyone should boast.

Ephesians 2:8, 9 NKJV

You therefore, my son, be strong in the grace that is in Christ Jesus.

2 Timothy 2:1 NKJV

But he gives us more grace. That is why Scripture says: "God opposes the proud but gives grace to the humble."

James 4:6

We have not earned our salvation; it is a gift from God. When we accept Christ as our savior, we are saved by God's grace. Let us praise God for His gift, and let us share the Good News with all who cross our paths.

The cross was heavy, the blood was real, and the price was extravagant. It would have bankrupted you or me, so he paid it for us. Call it simple. Call it a gift. But don't call it easy. Call it what it is. Call it grace.

Max Lucado

Accepting Your grace can be hard, Lord. Somehow, I feel that I must earn Your love and Your acceptance. Yet, the Bible makes this glorious promise: You love me and save me by Your grace. It is a gift I can only accept and cannot earn. Thank You for Your priceless, everlasting gift.

Amen

God's Love

The unfailing love of the Lord never ends!

Lamentations 3:22 NLT

Praise him, all you people of the earth, for he loves us with unfailing love; the faithfulness of the Lord endures forever.

Psalm 117:1-2 NLT

But God demonstrates his own love for us in this: While we were still sinners, Christ died for us.

Romans 5:8

His banner over me was love.

Song of Solomon 2:4 KJV

God is a loving Father. We are God's children, and we are called upon to be faithful to Him. We return our Father's love by sharing it with others. We honor our Heavenly Father by obeying His commandments and sharing His message. When we do, we are blessed…and the Father smiles.

I am convinced our hearts are not healthy until they have been satisfied by the only completely healthy love that exists: the love of God, Himself.

Beth Moore

God, You are love. I love You, Lord, because of Your great love for me. And, as I love You more, Lord, I am then able to love my family and friends more. Let me be Your loving servant, Heavenly Father, today and throughout eternity.

Amen

God's Mercy

Praise be to the God and Father of our Lord Jesus Christ! In his great mercy he has given us new birth into a living hope through the resurrection of Jesus Christ from the dead....

1 Peter 1:3

But because of his great love for us, God, who is rich in mercy, made us alive with Christ even when we were dead in transgressions—it is by grace you have been saved.

Ephesians 2:4,5

Speak and act as those who are going to be judged by the law that gives freedom, because judgment without mercy will be shown to anyone who has not been merciful. Mercy triumphs over judgment!

James 2:12,13

Cod is merciful, and His love is boundless and eternal. He sent His only Son to die for our sins. We must praise God always and thank Him for His gifts. One way that we thank God is to share His love and His mercy with all who cross our paths.

God's heart of mercy provides for us not only pardon from sin but a daily provision of spiritual food to strengthen us.

Jim Cymbala

Dear Lord, You have graced me with so much. You have blessed me with Your love and Your mercy. Enable me to be merciful toward others, Father, just as You have been merciful to me, and, today, let me share Your love with all whom I meet.

Amen

God's Plan

"For I know the plans that I have for you," declares the Lord, "plans to prosper you and not to harm you, plans to give you hope and a future. Then you will call upon me and come and pray to me, and I will listen to you."

Jeremiah 29:11-12

...it is God who works in you to will and to act according to his good purpose.

Philippians 2:13

In his heart a man plans his course, but the Lord determines his steps.

Proverbs 16:9

Unless the Lord builds a house, the work of the builders is useless.

Psalm 127:1 NLT

God has plans for you...big plans. To understand those plans, you must study God's Word and seek His will for your life. When you do, you'll be amazed at the marvelous things that an all-powerful, all-knowing God can do...and will do!

God manages perfectly, day and night, year in and year out, the movements of the stars, the wheeling of the planets, the staggering coordination of events that goes on at the molecular level in order to hold things together. There is no doubt that He can manage the timing of my days and weeks.

Elisabeth Elliot

Dear Lord, I am Your creation, and You created me for a reason. Give me the wisdom to follow Your direction for my life's journey. Let me do Your work here on earth by seeking Your will and living it, knowing that when I trust in You, Father, I am eternally blessed.

Amen

God's Power

Proclaim the power of God, whose majesty is over Israel, whose power is in the skies. You are awesome, O God, in your sanctuary; the God of Israel gives power and strength to his people. Praise be to God!

Psalm 68:34,35

Let every soul be subject unto the higher powers. For there is no power but of God: the powers that be are ordained of God.

Romans 13:1 KJV

Jesus looked at them and said, "With man this is impossible, but with God all things are possible."

Matthew 19:26

I pray...that you may know...his uncomparably great power for us who believe....

Ephesians 1:18,19

Many make the mistake of confusing activity with productivity. This is especially true among believers who are trying to serve God, but doing so in their own power. The inevitable result of man's busy-ness is burnout. God's work, empowered by God's Spirit, brings joy and peace. So, be active and involved in God's work, but don't depend upon your own resources. Instead, let Almighty God provide the power to accomplish the tasks He has chosen for you to do.

If we take God's program we can have God's power—not otherwise.

E. Stanley Jones

Lord, You give the work, and You give the power to accomplish Your work. Thank You for the challenges and opportunities of serving You every day. I pray, not that the task would be easy, but that You will empower me for the work You give me.

Amen

God's Support

Finally, be strong in the Lord and in his mighty power. Put on the full armor of God so that you can take your stand against the devil's schemes.

Ephesians 6:10-11

For the eyes of the Lord range throughout the earth to strengthen those whose hearts are fully committed to him.

2 Chronicles 16:9

Let not your heart be troubled; ye believe in God, believe also in me.

John 14:1 KJV

The Lord is good, a stronghold in the day of trouble, and He knows those who take refuge in Him.

Nahum 1:7 NASB

God loves us and protects us. In times of trouble, he comforts us; in times of sorrow, He dries our tears. When we are troubled, or weak, or sorrowful, God is as near as our next breath. Let us build our lives on the rock that cannot be shaken...let us trust in God.

He stands fast as your rock, steadfast as your safeguard, sleepless as your watcher, valiant as your champion.

C. H. Spurgeon

Heavenly Father, You never leave or forsake me. You are always with me, protecting me and encouraging me. Whatever this day may bring, I thank You for Your love and Your strength. Let me lean upon You, Father, this day and forever.

Amen

God's Timing

Humble yourselves, therefore, under God's mighty hand, that he may lift you up in due time.

1 Peter 5:6

To every thing there is a season, and a time to every purpose under the heaven: A time to be born, and a time to die; a time to plant, and a time to pluck up that which is planted; A time to kill, and a time to heal; a time to break down, and a time to build up; A time to weep, and a time to laugh; a time to mourn, and a time to dance; A time to cast away stones, and a time to gather stones together; a time to embrace, and a time to refrain from embracing; A time to get, and a time to lose; a time to keep, and a time to cast away; A time to rend, and a time to sew; a time to keep silence, and a time to speak; A time to love, and a time to hate; a time of war, and a time of peace.

Ecclesiastes 3:1-8 KJV

We human beings are impatient. We know what we want, and we know exactly when we want it: NOW! But, God knows better. He has created a world that unfolds according to His own timetable, not ours. Let us be patient as we wait for God to reveal the glorious plans that He has for our lives.

God never hurries. There are no deadlines against which He must work. To know this is to quiet our spirits and relax our nerves.

A. W. Tozer

Lord...Your timing is seldom my timing, but Your timing is always right for me. You are my Father, and You have a plan for my life that is grander than I can imagine. When I am impatient, remind me that You are never early or late. You are always on time, Lord, so let me trust in You...always.

Amen

Golden Rule

So in everything, do to others what you would have them do to you, for this sums up the Law and the Prophets.

Matthew 7:12

Don't be selfish....Be humble, thinking of others as better than yourself.

Philippians 2:3 NLT

As we have therefore opportunity, let us do good unto all men, especially unto them who are of the household of faith.

Galatians 6:10 KJV

And let us not be weary in well doing: for in due season we shall reap, if we faint not.

Galatians 6:9 KJV

The words of Matthew 7:12 remind us that, as believers in Christ, we are commanded to treat others as we wish to be treated. This commandment is, indeed, the Golden Rule for Christians of every generation. As we weave the thread of kindness into the very fabric of our lives, we give glory to the One who gave His life for us.

One of the most important phases of maturing is that of growth from self-centering to an understanding relationship to others. A person is not mature until he has both an ability and a willingness to see himself as one among others and to do unto those others as he would have them do to him.

Harry A. Overstreet

Heavenly Father...help me always to do for others as I would want others to do for me. Let me rejoice in their strengths, and enable me to overlook their weaknesses, just as they overlook mine. And, in all my dealings, may I be guided by the love of Christ that I feel in my heart.

Amen

Gratitude

Therefore, since we receive a kingdom which cannot be shaken, let us show gratitude by which we may offer to God an acceptable service with reverence and awe....

Hebrews 12:28 NASB

Make a joyful noise unto the Lord all ye lands. Serve the Lord with gladness: come before his presence with singing. Know ye that the Lord he is God: it is he that hath made us, and not we ourselves; we are his people and the sheep of his pasture. Enter into his gates with thanksgiving, and into his courts with praise; be thankful unto him and bless his name. For the Lord is good; his mercy is everlasting; and his truth endureth to all generations.

Psalm 100:1-5 KJV

And let the peace of God rule in your hearts...and be ye thankful.

Colossians 3:15 KJV

From childhood, we are taught to say "please" and "thank you." And, as adults, we should approach God in the same way. We should offer up our needs to Him in prayer ("Please, Dear Lord...."), and we should graciously give thanks for the gifts He has given us. Let us praise God and thank Him. He is the Giver of all things good.

A child of God should be a visible beatitude for joy and happiness, and a living doxology for gratitude and adoration.

Charles Spurgeon

Dear Lord, I want my attitude to be one of gratitude. You have given me so much; when I think of Your grace and goodness to me, I am humbled and thankful. Today, let me express my gratitude, Lord, not just through my words but also through my deeds, and may all the glory be Yours.

Amen

Grief

When I sit in darkness, the Lord shall be a light unto me.

Micah 7:8 KJV

The Lord is close to the brokenhearted and saves those who are crushed in spirit.

Psalm 34:18

...weeping may remain for a night, but rejoicing comes in the morning.

Psalm 30:5

God shall wipe away all the tears from their eyes.

Revelation 7:17 KJV

All of us experience adversity and pain. When we lose something—or someone—we love, we grieve our losses. During times of heartache—or heartbreak—we can turn to God for solace. When we do, He comforts us and, in time, He heals us.

The grace of God is sufficient for all our needs, for every problem and for every difficulty, for every broken heart, and for every human sorrow.

Peter Marshall

You have promised, Lord, that You will not give me any more than I can bear. You have promised to lift me out of my grief and despair. You have promised to put a new song on my lips. I thank You, Lord, for sustaining me in my day of sorrow. Restore me, and heal me, and use me as You will.

Amen

Hope

The Lord is good to those whose hope is in him, to the one who seeks him; it is good to wait quietly for the salvation of the Lord.

Lamentations 3:25-26

Happy is he...whose hope is in the Lord his God.

Psalm 146:5 KJV

Be of good courage, and he shall strengthen your heart, all ye that hope in the Lord.

Psalm 31:24 KJV

Now the God of hope fill you with all joy and peace in believing, that ye may abound in hope.

Romans 15:13 KJV

This world can be a place of trials and tribulations, but as believers we are secure. We need never lose hope because God has promised us peace, joy, and eternal life. So, let us face each day with hope in our hearts and trust in our God. After all, God has promised us that we are His throughout eternity, and he keeps His promises.

No other religion, no other philosophy promises new bodies, hearts, and minds. Only in the Gospel of Christ do hurting people find such incredible hope.

Joni Eareckson Tada

Today, Dear Lord, I will live in hope. If I become discouraged, I will turn to You. If I grow weary, I will seek strength in You. In every aspect of my life, I will trust You. You are my Father, Lord, and I place my hope and my faith in You.

Amen

Humility

Humble yourselves, therefore, under God's mighty hand, that he may lift your up in due time.

1 Peter 5:6

...This is the one I [God] esteem: he who is humble and contrite in spirit, and trembles at my word.

Isaiah 66:2

He has showed you, O man, what is good. And what does the LORD require of you? To act justly and to love mercy and to walk humbly with your God.

Micah 6:8

And he said to them: "I tell you the truth, unless you change and become like little children, you will never enter the kingdom of heaven. Therefore, whoever humbles himself like this child is the greatest in heaven."

Matthew 18:3-4

Dietrich Bonhoeffer was correct when he observed, "It is very easy to overestimate the importance of our own achievements in comparison with what we owe others." In other words, reality breeds humility. So, instead of puffing out your chest and saying, "Look at me!", give credit where credit is due, starting with God. And, rest assured: There is no such thing as a self-made man. All of us are made by God...and He deserves the glory, not us.

Let us humble our hearts before the Lord and seek his help and approval above all other things.

Jim Cymbala

Heavenly Father, Jesus clothed Himself with humility when He chose to leave heaven and come to earth to live and die for all creation. Lord, He is my Master and my example. Clothe me with humility, Lord, so that I might be more like Your Son. And, keep me mindful, Lord, that You are the giver and sustainer of life, and to You goes the glory and the praise.

Amen

Jesus Christ the same yesterday, and to-day, and for ever.

Hebrews 13:8 KGV

Therefore if any man be in Christ, he is a new creature: old things are passed away; behold, all things are become new.

2 Corinthians 5:17 KGV

The next day John seeth Jesus coming unto him, and saith, Behold the Lamb of God, which taketh away the sin of the world.

John 1:29 KGV

In the beginning was the Word, and the Word was with God, and the Word was God....And the Word was made flesh, and dwelt among us, (and we beheld his glory, the glory as of the only begotten of the Father,) full of grace and truth.

John 1:1,14 KGV

The old familiar hymn begins, "What a friend we have in Jesus...." No truer words were ever penned. Jesus is the sovereign friend and ultimate savior of mankind. Christ showed enduring love for His believers by willingly sacrificing His own life so that we might have eternal life. Let us love Him, praise Him, and share His message of salvation with our neighbors and with the world.

Abide in Jesus, the sinless one—which means, give up all of self and its life, and dwell in God's will and rest in His strength. This is what brings the power that does not commit sin.

Andrew Murray

Jesus, Jesus...Lord, there is just something about His name. He is the name above all names, and one day every knee will bow and every tongue confess Him Lord. Jesus is the sweetest name I know.

Amen

Joy

These things have I spoken unto you, that my joy might remain in you, and that your joy might be full.

John 15:11 KJV

But let all who take refuge in you be glad; let them sing for joy. Spread your protection over them, that those who love your name may rejoice in you.

Psalm 5:11

So now we can rejoice in our wonderful new relationship with God—all because of what our Lord Jesus Christ has done for us in making us friends of God.

Romans 5:11 NLT

Christ made it clear to His followers: He intended that His joy would become their joy. And it still holds true today: Christ intends that His believers share His love, His peace, and His joy. Today, let us celebrate our Savior and share His joy with others just as He freely shares His love and His joy with us.

A life of intimacy with God is characterized by joy.

Oswald Chambers

Father, You have created a glorious universe that is far beyond my understanding. You have given me the gift of Your Son and the gift of salvation. Let me be a joyful Christian, Lord, this day and every day. Today is Your gift to me. Let me use it to Your glory while giving all the praise to You.

Amen

Kindness

And be ye kind one to another, tender-hearted, forgiving one another, even as God for Christ's sake hath forgiven you.

Ephesians 4:32 KJV

O God, thou art my God; early will I seek thee: my soul thirsteth for thee, my flesh longeth for thee in a dry and thirsty land, where no water is; To see thy power and thy glory, so as I have seen thee in the sanctuary. Because thy lovingkindness is better than life, my lips shall praise thee.

Psalm 63:1-3 KJV

A kind man benefits himself...

Proverbs 11:17

...Verily I say unto you, Inasmuch as ye have done it unto one of the least of these my brethren, ye have done it unto me.

Matthew 25:40 KJV

If we are to follow the commands of our Lord and savior, we must sow seeds of kindness wherever we go. Kindness is God's way. It should be ours, too. So, today, let's be a little kinder than necessary, and let's teach our families and friends the art of kindness through our words and our deeds. People are watching…and so is God.

Do all the good you can. By all the means you can. In all the ways you can. In all the places you can. At all the times you can. To all the people you can. As long as ever you can.

John Wesley

Heavenly Father, sometimes this world can become a demanding place, a place where I rush through the day with my eyes focused only on my next step. Slow me down, Lord, and give me wisdom and peace so that I might look beyond my own needs and see the needs of those around me. Today, help me to be generous, compassionate, and understanding. And, let me show kindness to all who need the healing touch of our Master's hand.

Amen

Loving God

Whoever does not love does not know God, because God is love.

1 John 4:8

This is love: not that we loved God, but that he loved us and sent his Son as an atoning sacrifice for our sins.

1 John 4:10

I will sing of the LORD'S great love forever; with my mouth I will make your faithfulness known through all generations.

Psalm 89:1

And we know that all things work together for good to them that love God, to them who are the called according to his purpose.

Romans 8:28 KJV

C. S. Lewis once observed, "A man's spiritual health is exactly proportional to his love for God." If we are to enjoy the spiritual health that God intends for our lives, we must praise Him and love Him. And, this is as it should be…after all, He first loved us.

Everything in your Christian life, everything about knowing Him and experiencing Him, everything about knowing His will, depends on the quality of your love relationship to God.

Henry Blackaby

Dear Heavenly Father, You have blessed me with a love that is infinite and eternal. Let me love You, Lord, more and more each day. Make me a loving servant, Dear Lord, today and throughout eternity. And, let me show my love for You by sharing Your message and Your love with others.

Amen

Loving Others

But now faith, hope, love, abide these three; but the greatest of these is love.

1 Corinthians 13:13 NASB

He that loveth his brother abideth in the light, and there is none occasion of stumbling in him.

1 John 2:10 KJV

If a man say, I love God, and hateth his brother, he is a liar: for he that loveth not his brother whom he hath seen, how can he love God whom he hath not seen?

1 John 4:20 KJV

By this all men will know that you are my disciples, if you love one another.

John 13:35

The familiar words of 1 Corinthians 13 remind us that love is God's commandment. Faith is important, of course. So, too, is hope. But love is more important still. Christ showed His love for us on the cross, and, as Christians, we are called upon to return Christ's love by sharing it. Today, let us spread Christ's love by word and by example. And the greatest of these, of course, is example.

To love another person is to help them love God.

Søren Kierkegaard

Father...You have given me love that is beyond human understanding, and I am Your loving servant. May the love that I feel for You be reflected in the compassion that I show toward others. Give me Your eyes to see others as You see them, Lord, and let me show compassion and understanding to those who cross my path this day and every day.

Amen

Maturity

But grow in the grace and knowledge of our Lord and Savior Jesus Christ.

2 Peter 3:18

When I was child, I spake as a child, I understood as a child, I thought as a child; but when I became a man, I put away childish things.

1 Corinthians 13:11 KJV

Therefore let us leave the elementary teachings about Christ and go on to maturity....

Hebrews 6:1

...he who began a good work in you will carry it on to completion until the day of Christ Jesus.

Philippians 1:6

Norman Vincent Peale had powerful advice for Christians of all ages: "Ask the God who made you to keep remaking you." When we cease to grow, either emotionally or spiritually, we do ourselves a profound disservice. Instead, we should continue to grow every day of our lives. We do so by studying God's Word and living in His will. As we do, we are blessed.

A Christian is never in a state of completion but always in the process of becoming.

Martin Luther

Thank You, Lord, that I am not yet what I am to become. The Holy Scripture says that You are at work in my life, continuing to help me grow and to mature in the faith. Show me Your wisdom, Lord, and let me live according to Your Word and Your will.

Amen

Miracles

You are the God who performs miracles;
you display your power among the peoples.

Psalm 77:14

...Jesus said to them, "I have shown you
many great miracles from the Father."

John 10:32

God also testified to it [salvation] by
signs, wonders and various miracles, and
gifts of the Holy Spirit distributed according to his will.

Hebrews 2:4

For with God nothing shall be impossible.

Luke 1:37 KJV

We are imperfect human beings with limited understanding and limited faith, and, thus, we sometimes place limitations on God. But God's power has no limitations. God is a worker of miracles both great and small, and when we trust Him with everything we have and everything we are, we experience the miraculous results of His endless love and His awesome power.

We have a God who delights in impossibilities.

Andrew Murray

Dear God, nothing is impossible for You. Your infinite power is beyond human understanding. Keep me always mindful of Your strength. When I lose hope, give me faith; when others lose hope, let me tell them of Your glory and Your works. Today, Lord, let me expect the miraculous, and let me trust in You.

Amen

Missions

"Come, follow me," Jesus said, "and I will make you fishers of men."

Mark 1:17

But ye shall receive power, after that the Holy Ghost is come upon you: and ye shall be witnesses unto me both in Jerusalem, and in all Judea, and in Samaria, and unto the uttermost part of the earth.

Acts 1:8 KJV

After these things the Lord appointed other seventy also, and sent them two and two before his face into every city and place, whither he himself would come. Therefore said he unto them, The harvest truly is great, but the laborers are few: pray ye therefore the Lord of the harvest, that he would send forth laborers into his harvest. Go your ways: behold, I send you forth as lambs among wolves.

Luke 10:1-3 KJV

As believers, we are called to share the Good News of Jesus Christ with our families, our neighbors, and the world. Jesus commanded His disciples to become fishers of men. We must do likewise. And, the time to go fishing is now.

The Christian life is a matter of coming and going: "Come unto me..." (Matt. 11:28); Go ye unto the world..." (Mark 16:15).

Vance Havner

Heavenly Father, every man and woman, every boy and girl is Your child. You desire that all Your children know Jesus as their Lord and Savior. Father, let me be part of Your Great Commission. Let me give, let me pray, and let me go out into this world so that I might be a fisher of men...for You.

Amen

Mistakes

Therefore if any man be in Christ, he is a new creature: old things are passed away; behold, all things are become new.

2 Corinthians 5:17 KJV

If we confess our sins, he is faithful and just and will forgive us our sins and purify us from all unrighteousness.

1 John 1:9

I will instruct you and teach you in the way you should go; I will counsel you and watch over you.

Psalm 32:8

He who conceals his sins does not prosper, but whoever confesses and renounces them finds mercy.

Proverbs 28:13

The words are all too familiar and all too true: "To err is human…." Yes, we human beings are inclined to make mistakes, and lots of them. When we commit the inevitable blunders of life, let us be quick to correct our errors. And, when we are hurt by the mistakes of others, let us be quick to forgive, just as God has forgiven us.

The only real mistake is one from which we learn nothing, and I think I have learned much…. But I think we must be patient with ourselves, just as God is infinitely patient with us.

John Powell

Lord, I know that I am imperfect and that I fail You in many ways. Thank You for Your forgiveness and for Your unconditional love. Show me the error of my ways, Lord, that I might confess my wrongdoing and correct my mistakes. And, let me grow each day in wisdom, and in faith, and in my love for You.

Amen

Optimism

I can do everything through him that gives me strength.

Philippians 4:13

Finally, brethren, whatsoever things are true, whatsoever things are honest, whatsoever things are just, whatsoever things are pure, whatsoever things are lovely, whatsoever things are of good report; if there be any virtue, and if there be any praise, think on these things.

Philippians 4:8 KJV

Make me to hear joy and gladness....

Psalm 51:8 KJV

The Lord is my light and my salvation; whom shall I fear? The Lord is the strength of my life; of whom shall I be afraid?

Psalm 27:1 KJV

Christians have every reason to be optimistic about life. As John Calvin observed, "There is not one blade of grass, there is no color in this world that is not intended to make us rejoice." Today, think optimistically about yourself and your world. And, share your optimism with others. You'll be better for it...and so will they.

The essence of optimism is that it takes no account of the present, but it is a source of inspiration, of vitality and hope where others have resigned; it enables a man to hold his head high, to claim the future for himself and not abandon it to his enemy.

Dietrich Bonhoeffer

Lord, fill me with your expectations. Let me expect the best from You, and let me look for the best in others. If I become discouraged, Lord, turn my thoughts and my prayers to You. I trust You, Lord, to direct my life. Empower me to be Your faithful, hopeful, optimistic servant every day that I live.

Amen

Patience

Be still before the Lord and wait patiently for him....

Psalm 37:7

For when the way is rough, your patience has a chance to grow. So let it grow, and don't try to squirm out of your problems.

James 1:3,4a TLB

The Lord is wonderfully good to those who wait for him and seek him. So it is good to wait quietly for salvation from the Lord.

Lamentations 3:25-26 NLT

Wait on the LORD: be of good courage, and he shall strengthen thine heart: wait, I say, on the LORD.

Psalm 27:14 KJV

Psalm 37:7 commands us to wait patiently for God, but, for most of us, waiting quietly for Him is difficult. Why? Because we are fallible human beings. Still, God instructs us to be patient in all things, and that's as it should be. After all, think how patient God has been with us.

Teach us, O Lord, the disciplines of patience, for to wait is often harder than to work.

Peter Marshall

Dear Heavenly Father, let me wait quietly for You. Let me live according to Your plan and according to Your timetable. When I am hurried, slow me down. When I become impatient with others, give me empathy. Today, I want to be a patient Christian, Dear Lord, as I trust in You and in Your master plan.

Amen

Peace

Peace I leave with you, my peace I give unto you: not as the world giveth, give I unto you. Let not your heart be troubled, neither let it be afraid.

John 14:27 KJV

God has called us to live in peace.

1 Corinthians 7:15

And let the peace of God rule in your hearts...and be ye thankful.

Colossians 3:15 KJV

Thou wilt keep him in perfect peace, whose mind is stayed on thee.

Isaiah 26:3 KJV

The timeless words of John 14:27 give us hope: Jesus offers us peace, not as the world gives, but as He alone gives. We, as believers, can accept His peace and be transformed. Today, as a gift to yourself, to your family, and to your friends, claim the inner peace that is your spiritual birthright: the peace of Jesus Christ. It is offered freely; it has been paid for in full; it is yours for the asking. So ask. And then share.

The peace that Jesus gives is never engineered by circumstances on the outside.

Oswald Chambers

Lord, when I turn my thoughts and prayers to You, I feel the peace that You intend for my life. When I am worried or anxious, Lord, turn my thoughts back to You. You are the Giver of all things good, Dear Lord, and You give me peace when I draw close to You. Help me to trust Your will, to follow Your commands, and to accept Your peace, today and forever.

Amen

Perseverance

I have fought a good fight, I have finished my course, I have kept the faith.

2 Timothy 4:7 KJV

Let us not become weary in doing good, for at the proper time we will reap a harvest if we do not give up.

Galatians 6:9

You need to persevere so that when you have done the will of God, you will receive what he has promised.

Hebrews 10:36

...I do not consider myself yet to have taken hold of it. But one thing I do: Forgetting what is behind and straining toward what is ahead, I press on toward the goal to win the prize for which God has called me heavenward in Christ Jesus.

Philippians 3:13,14

The old saying is as true today as it was when it was first spoken: "Life is a marathon, not a sprint." Life, indeed, requires perseverance, so wise travelers select a traveling companion who never tires and never falters. That partner, of course, is God. Are you tired? Ask God for strength. Are you discouraged? Believe in His promises. Are you defeated? Pray as if everything depended upon God, and work as if everything depended upon yourself. With God's help, you can persevere...and you will.

By perseverance the snail reached the Ark.

Charles Spurgeon

Lord, sometimes, life is difficult indeed. Sometimes, we are burdened or fearful. Sometimes, we cry tears of bitterness or loss, but even then, You never leave our sides. Today, Lord, let me be a finisher of my faith. Let me persevere—even if the day is difficult—and let me follow Your Son Jesus Christ this day and forever.

Amen

Praise

I will praise thee, O LORD, with my whole heart; I will show forth all thy marvelous works. I will be glad and rejoice in thee: I will sing praise to thy name, O thou Most High.

Psalm 9:1-2 KJV

Make a joyful noise unto God, all ye lands: sing forth the honor of his name: make his praise glorious.

Psalm 66:1-2 KJV

Through Him then, let us continually offer up a sacrifice of praise to God, that is, the fruit of lips that give thanks to His name.

Hebrews 13:15 NASB

The LORD is my strength and song, and He has become my salvation; He is my God, and I will praise Him....

Exodus 15:2 NKJV

POWER PROMISES AND PRAYERS

When is the best time to praise God? In church? Before dinner is served? When we tuck little children into bed? All of the above, and more. The best time to praise God is all day, every day, to the greatest extent we can, with thanksgiving in our hearts and with a song on our lips. Today, find a little more time to lift your thankful heart to God in prayer. You owe Him everything, including your praise.

Praise...reestablishes the proper chain of command; we recognize that the King is on the throne and that he has saved his people.

Max Lucado

Lord, Your hand created the smallest grain of sand and the grandest stars in the heavens. You watch over Your entire creation, and You watch over me. Thank You, Lord, for loving this world so much that You sent Your Son to die for our sins. I am grateful for the priceless gift of Your Son, and I praise Your holy name forever.

Amen

Prayer

Rejoice evermore. Pray without ceasing. In every thing give thanks: for this is the will of God in Christ Jesus concerning you.

1 Thessalonians 5:16-18 KJV

The effective prayer of a righteous man can accomplish much.

James 5:16 NASB

...for your Father knows what you need, before you ask Him.

Matthew 6:8 NASB

If you believe, you will receive whatever you ask for in prayer.

Matthew 21:22

Prayer changes things and it changes us. Today, instead of turning things over in your mind, turn them over to God in prayer. Instead of worrying about your next decision, decide to let God lead the way. Don't limit your prayers to meals or to bedtime. Pray constantly about things great and small. God is listening, and He wants to hear from you. Now.

God is always listening.

Stormie Omartian

I pray to You, heavenly Father, because You desire it and because I need it. Prayer not only changes things, but, more importantly, it changes me. Help me, Lord, never to face the demands of the day without first spending time with You.

Amen

Righteousness

For the eyes of the Lord are over the righteous, and his ears are open unto their prayers: but the face of the Lord is against them that do evil.

1 Peter 3:12 KJV

Blessed are those who hunger and thirst for righteousness, for they will be filled.

Matthew 5:6

Teach me to do thy will; for thou art my God: thy Spirit is good; lead me into the land of uprightness.

Psalm 143:10 KJV

The LORD rewarded me according to my righteousness....

Psalm 18:20 KJV

God has given us a guidebook for righteous living called the Holy Bible. It contains thorough instructions which, if followed, lead to fulfillment, righteousness and salvation. As Christians, we are called to study God's Word and to live by it. Embrace righteousness. And, for further instructions—read the manual.

We must appropriate the tender mercy of God every day after conversion, or problems quickly develop. We need his grace daily in order to live a righteous life.

Jim Cymbala

Holy, Holy, Holy...You are a Righteous and Holy God who commands that I seek to be holy and righteous. Forgive me when I fall short, Lord, and renew a right spirit within me. Let me serve You and obey the teachings of Your Word. Lead me far from temptation, Father, and guide me in Your will for my life.

Amen

Salvation

My dear children, I write this to you so that you will not sin. But if anybody does sin, we have one who speaks to the Father in our defense—Jesus Christ, the Righteous One. He is the atoning sacrifice for our sins, and not only for ours but also for the sins of the whole world.

1 John 2:1,2

It is by the name of Jesus Christ of Nazareth...Salvation is found in no one else, for there is no other name under heaven given to men by which we must be saved.

Acts 4:10,12

The LORD is my strength and my song; he has become my salvation. He is my God, and I will praise him, my father's God, and I will exalt him.

Exodus 15:2

The familiar words of Ephesians 2:8 make God's promise perfectly clear: For it is by grace we have been saved, through faith. We are saved not because of our good deeds but because of our faith in Christ. May we, who have been given so much, praise our Savior for the gift of salvation, and may we share the joyous news of our Master's love and His grace.

If I can lead but one lost human to the personhood of Jesus Christ, the giver of life itself, then I need no other justification for my earthly existence.

James Dobson

Lord, I am only here on this earth for a brief while. But, You have offered me the priceless gift of eternal life through Your Son Jesus. I accept Your gift, Lord, with thanksgiving and praise. Enable me to share the good news of my salvation with those who need Your healing touch.

Amen

Seeking God

God did this so that men would seek him and perhaps reach out for him and find him, though he is not far from each one of us.

Acts 17:27

This is what the LORD says to the house of Israel: "Seek me and live...."

Amos 5:4

But if from there you seek the LORD your God, you will find him if you look for him with all your heart and with all your soul.

Deuteronomy 4:29

But without faith it is impossible to please him: for he that cometh to God must believe that he is, and that he is a rewarder of them that diligently seek him.

Hebrews 11:6 KJV

Where is God? He is everywhere you have ever been and everywhere you will ever go. He is with you night and day; He knows your every thought; He hears your every heartbeat. When you earnestly seek Him, you will find Him because He is here, waiting patiently for you to reach out to Him…right here…right now.

Don't take anyone else's word for God. Find him for yourself, and then you too will know, by the wonderful, warm tug on your heartstrings, that he is there for sure.

Billy Graham

How comforting it is, Dear Lord, to know that if I seek You, I will find You. You are with me, Lord, every step I take. Let me reach out to You, and let me praise You for revealing Your Word, Your way, and Your love.

Amen

Serving God

And now, O Israel, what does the LORD your God ask of you but to fear the LORD your God, to walk in all his ways, to love him, to serve the LORD your God with all your heart and with all your soul....

Deuteronomy 10:12

...choose you this day whom ye will serve...as for me and my house, we will serve the LORD.

Joshua 24:15 KJV

No servant can serve two masters. Either he will hate the one and love the other, or he will be devoted to the one and despise the other. You cannot serve both God and Money.

Luke 16:13

Your attitude should be the same as that of Christ Jesus Who...made himself nothing, taking the very nature of a servant....

Philippians 2:5-7

When Jesus was tempted by Satan, the Master's response was unambiguous. Jesus chose to worship the Lord and serve him only (Matthew 4:10). We, as followers of Christ, must follow in His footsteps. When we place God in a position of secondary importance, we do ourselves great harm. But, when we imitate Jesus and place the Lord in His rightful place—at the center of our lives—then we claim spiritual treasures that will endure forever.

God wants us to serve Him with a willing spirit, one that would choose no other way.

Beth Moore

Lord, I can serve only one master; let me serve You. Let my actions be pleasing to You; let my words reflect Your infinite love; let my prayers be sincere and my thoughts be pure. In everything that I do, Father, let me praise You and serve You today and for eternity.

Amen

Serving Others

A generous man will prosper; he who refreshes others will himself be refreshed.

Proverbs 11:25

Be devoted to one another in brotherly love. Honor one another above yourselves.

Romans 12:10

Whatever you do, work at it with all your heart, as working for the Lord, not for men, since you know that you will receive an inheritance from the Lord as a reward. It is the Lord Christ you are serving.

Colossians 3:23,24

But a Samaritan, as he traveled, came where the man was; and when he saw him, he took pity on him. He went to him and bandaged his wounds, pouring on oil and wine. Then he put the man on his own donkey, took him to an inn and took care of him.

Luke 10:33,34

The teachings of Jesus are quite clear: We achieve greatness through service to others. But, as weak human beings, we sometimes fall short as we seek to puff ourselves up and glorify our own accomplishments. Jesus commands otherwise. If we seek spiritual greatness, we must first become servants.

Christians are like the several flowers in a garden that have each of them the dew of heaven, which, being shaken by the wind, they let fall at each other's roots, whereby they are jointly nourished, and become nourishers of each other.

John Bunyan

Dear Father in heaven…when Jesus humbled Himself and became a servant, He also became an example for His followers. Today, as I serve my family and friends, I do so in the name of Jesus, my Lord and Master. Guide my steps, Father, and let my service be pleasing to You.

Amen

Strength

I can do all things through Him who strengthens me.

Philippians 4:13 NASB

...but those who hope in the LORD will renew their strength. They will soar on wings like eagles; they will run and not grow weary, they will walk and not be faint.

Isaiah 40:31

He said unto me, My grace is sufficient for thee: for my strength is made perfect in weakness.

2 Corinthians 12:9 KJV

The LORD is my strength and my song....

Exodus 15:2

God is a infinite source of strength and courage for those who call upon Him. When we are weary, He gives us strength. When we see no hope, God reminds us of His promises. When we grieve, God wipes away our tears. Whatever our circumstances, God will protect us and care for us...if we let Him.

God gives us always strength enough, and sense enough, for everything he wants us to do.

John Ruskin

Lord, sometimes life is difficult. Sometimes, I am worried, weary, or heartbroken. But, when I lift my eyes to You, Father, You strengthen me. When I am weak, You lift me up. Today, I turn to You, Lord, for my strength and my salvation.

Amen

Talents

Now there are varieties of gifts, but the same Spirit. And there are varieties of ministries, and the same Lord.

1 Corinthians 12:4-5 NASB

Do not neglect the spiritual gift that is within you....

1 Timothy 4:14 NASB

Every good gift and every perfect gift is from above, and cometh down from the Father of lights.

James 1:17 KJV

The old saying is both familiar and true: "What we are is God's gift to us; what we become is our gift to God." Each of us possesses special talents, gifted by God, that can be nurtured carefully or ignored totally. Our challenge, of course, is to use our abilities to the greatest extent possible. Our talents are priceless gifts from God, and the way that we say "thank you" for God's gifts is to use them.

One thing taught large in the Holy Scriptures is that while God gives His gifts freely, He will require a strict accounting of them at the end of the road. Each man is personally responsible for his store, be it large or small, and will be required to explain his use of it before the judgment seat of Christ.

A. W. Tozer

Lord, You have given me abilities to be used for the glory of Your kingdom. Give me the courage and the perseverance to use those talents. Keep me mindful that all my gifts come from You, Lord. Let me be Your faithful, humble servant, and let me give You all the glory and all the praise.

Amen

Temptation

For we do not have a high priest who is unable to sympathize with our weaknesses, but we have one who has been tempted in every way, just as we are—yet was without sin.

Hebrews 4:15

There hath no temptation taken you but such as is common to man: but God is faithful, who will not suffer you to be tempted above that ye are able; but will with the temptation also make a way to escape, that ye may be able to bear it.

1 Corinthians 10:13 KJV

...be vigilant; because your adversary the devil, as a roaring lion, walketh about, seeking whom he may devour.

1 Peter 5:8 KJV

Blessed is the man that endureth temptation: for when he is tried, he shall receive the crown of life....

James 1:12 KJV

How hard is it to run into temptation in this crazy world? The devil, it seems, is working overtime these days, and causing pain and heartache in more places and in more ways than ever before. As Christians, we must remain vigilant. Not only must we resist Satan when he confronts us, but we must also avoid those places where Satan can most easily tempt us. As believing Christians, we must beware, and we must earnestly wrap ourselves in the protection of God's Holy Word. When we do, we are secure.

Because Christ has faced our every temptation without sin, we never face a temptation that has no door of escape.

Beth Moore

Lord, life is filled with temptations to stray from Your chosen path. But, I face no temptation that You have not already met and conquered through my Lord and Savior Jesus Christ. He has been victorious over the devil's temptations, and He empowers me with the same strength to overcome.

Amen

Testimony

...sanctify the Lord God in your hearts: and be ready always to give an answer to every man that asketh you a reason of the hope that is in you....

1 Peter 3:15 KJV

And I say to you, everyone who confesses Me before men, the Son of Man will confess him also before the angels of God....

Luke 12:8 NASB

Whatever I tell you in the dark, speak in the light; and what you hear in the ear, preach on the housetops.

Matthew 10:27 NKJV

We are therefore Christ's ambassadors, as though God were making his appeal through us. We implore you on Christ's behalf: Be reconciled to God.

2 Corinthians 5:20

In his second letter to Timothy, Paul shares a message to believers of every generation when he writes, "God has not given us a spirit of timidity." Paul's meaning is clear: When sharing our testimonies, we, as Christians, must be courageous, forthright, and unashamed.

I still believe we ought to talk about Jesus. The old country doctor of my boyhood days always began his examination by saying, "Let me see your tongue." That's a good way to check a Christian: the tongue test— let's hear what he is talking about.

Vance Havner

Dear Lord, the life that I live and the words that I speak bear testimony to my faith. Make me be a faithful servant of Your Son Jesus. Let my testimony be worthy of You: Let my words be sure and true, Lord, and let my actions point others to You.

Amen

Thanksgiving

It is good to give thanks to the Lord, to sing praises to the Most High. It is good to proclaim your unfailing love in the morning, your faithfulness in the evening.

Psalm 92:1-2 NLT

I will thank you, Lord, with all my heart; I will tell of all the marvelous things you have done. I will be filled with joy because of you. I will sing praises to your name, O Most High.

Psalm 9:1-2 NLT

Give thanks in all circumstances; for this is God's will for you in Christ Jesus.

1 Thessalonians 5:18

And let the peace of God rule in your hearts...and be ye thankful.

Colossians 3:15 KJV

Sometimes, in the crush of everyday living, we simply don't stop long enough to pause and thank our Creator for the countless blessings He has bestowed upon us. But, when we neglect our God, we suffer. God has blessed us beyond measure, and we owe Him everything, including our praise. Let us praise Him always.

It is only with gratitude that life becomes rich.

Dietrich Bonhoeffer

Dear Heavenly Father, Your gifts are greater than I can imagine, and Your love for me is greater than I can fathom. May I live each day with thanksgiving in my heart and praise on my lips. Thank You for the gift of Your Son and for the promise of eternal life. Let me share the joyous news of Jesus Christ with a world that desperately needs His healing touch this day and every day.

Amen

Today

For he says, "In the time of my favor I heard you, and in the day of salvation I helped you." I tell you, now is the time of God's favor, now is the day of salvation.

2 Corinthians 6:2

Give your entire attention to what God is doing right now, and don't get worked up about what may or may not happen tomorrow. God will help you deal with whatever hard things come up when the time comes.

Matthew 6:33,34 MSG

This is the day the Lord has made; let us rejoice and be glad in it.

Psalm 118:24

...encourage one another daily, as long as it is Today....

Hebrews 3:13

There's an old saying—trite but true— "Today is the first day of the rest of your life." Whatever the days ahead may hold, keep God as your partner and Christ as your Savior. And every day, give thanks to the One who created you and saved you. God's love for you is infinite. Accept it joyously and be thankful.

"Suzanne will not be at school today," I once wrote to her teacher. "She stayed at home to play with her mother." I don't remember many other days of her elementary years. But I remember that day.

Gloria Gaither

Help me, Father, to learn from the past but not live in it. And, help me to plan for the future but not to worry about it. This is the day You have given me, Lord. Let me use it according to Your master plan, and let me give thanks for Your blessings. Empower me to live each moment to the fullest, totally involved in Your will.

Amen

Trusting God

Do not let your hearts be troubled. Trust in God; trust also in me. In my Father's house are many rooms; if it were not so, I would have told you. I am going there to prepare a place for you.

John 14:1,2

It is better to trust in the LORD than to put confidence in man. It is better to trust in the LORD than to put confidence in princes.

Psalm 118:8-9 KJV

The LORD is my rock, and my fortress, and my deliverer; my God, my strength, in whom I will trust....

Psalm 18:2 KJV

He heeded their prayer, because they put their trust in him.

1 Chronicles 5:20 NKJV

Do you aspire to do great things for God's kingdom? Then trust Him with every aspect of your life. Trust Him with your relationships. Trust Him with your finances. Follow His commandments and pray for His guidance. Then, wait patiently for God's revelations and for His blessings. In His own fashion and in His own time, God will bless you in ways that you never could have imagined.

Either we are adrift in chaos or we are individuals, created, loved, upheld and placed purposefully, exactly where we are. Can you believe that? Can you trust God for that?

Elisabeth Elliot

Lord, when I trust in things of this earth, I will be disappointed. But, when I put my faith in You, I am secure. You are my rock and my shield. Upon Your firm foundation I will build my life. When I am worried, let me trust in You. You will love me and protect me, and You will share Your boundless grace today, tomorrow, and forever.

Amen

Truth

Jesus answered, "I am the way and the truth and the life. No one comes to the Father except through me."

John 14:6

To this end was I born, and for this cause came I into the world, that I should bear witness unto the truth.

John 18:37 KJV

These are the things you are to do: Speak the truth to each other, and render true and sound judgment in your courts....

Zechariah 8:16

... as we have received mercy, we faint not; but have renounced the hidden things of dishonesty, not walking in craftiness, nor handling the word of God deceitfully; but, by manifestation of the truth, commending ourselves to every man's conscience in the sight of God.

2 Corinthians 4:1-2 KJV

The words of John 8:32 are both profound and familiar: "Ye shall know the truth, and the truth shall make you free." Truth is God's way: He commands His children to live in truth, and He rewards those who follow his commandment. Jesus is the personification of a perfect, liberating truth that offers salvation to mankind. Do you seek to walk with God? Then you must walk in truth, and you must walk with the Savior.

Those who walk in truth walk in liberty.
Beth Moore

Dear Lord, Jesus said He was the truth, and I believe Him. Lord, may Jesus always be the standard for truth in my life, so that I might be a worthy example to others and a worthy servant to You.
Amen

Wisdom

Let the word of Christ dwell in you richly in all wisdom; teaching and admonishing one another in psalms and hymns and spiritual songs, singing with grace in your hearts to the Lord.

Colossians 3:16 KJV

If any of you lack wisdom, let him ask of God, that giveth to all men liberally, and upbraideth not; and it shall be given him.

James 1:5 KJV

...the wisdom that is from above is first pure, then peaceable, gentle, and easy to be entreated, full of mercy and good fruits, without partiality, and without hypocrisy.

James 3:17 KJV

For the LORD giveth wisdom: out of his mouth cometh knowledge and understanding.

Proverbs 2:6 KJV

Wisdom is like a savings account: If you add to it consistently, then eventually you'll have a great sum. The secret to success is consistency. Do you seek wisdom? Then seek it every day, and seek it in the right place. That place, of course, is God's Holy Word.

Don't expect wisdom to come into your life like great chunks of rock on a conveyor belt. Wisdom comes privately from God as a byproduct of right decisions, godly reactions, and the application of spiritual principles to daily circumstances.

Chuck Swindoll

I seek wisdom, Lord, not as the world gives, but as You give. Lead me in Your ways and teach me from Your Word so that, in time, my wisdom might glorify Your kingdom, Lord, and Your Son.

Amen

Work

...but I laboured more abundantly than they all: yet not I, but the grace of God which was with me.

1 Corinthians 15:10 KJV

He did it with all his heart, and prospered.

2 Chronicles 31:21 KJV

Work hard so God can say to you, "Well done." Be a good workman, one who does not need to be ashamed when God examines your work....

2 Timothy 2:15 TLB

...My heart took delight in all my work....

Ecclesiastes 2:10

It has been said that there are no short-cuts to any place worth going to. Hard work is not simply a proven way to get ahead, it's also part of God's plan for His children. God did not create us for lives of mediocrity; He created us for far greater things. Earning great things usually requires work and lots of it, which is perfectly fine with God. After all, He knows that we're up to the task, and He has big plans for us. Very big plans...

I long to accomplish a great and noble task, but it is my chief duty to accomplish small tasks as if they were great and noble.

Helen Keller

Heavenly Father, I seek to be Your faithful servant. When I am tired, give me strength. When I become frustrated, give me patience. When I lose sight of Your purpose for my life, give me a passion for my daily responsibilities, and when I have completed my work, let all the honor and glory be Yours.

Amen

Worry

Let not your heart be troubled: ye believe in God, believe also in me.

John 14:1 KJV

Cast your burden upon the Lord and He will sustain you: He will never allow the righteous to be shaken.

Psalm 55:22 NASB

An anxious heart weighs a man down....

Proverbs 12:25

So, don't be anxious about tomorrow. God will take care of your tomorrow too. Live one day at a time.

Matthew 6:34 TLB

Are you worried? Take your worries to God. Are you troubled? Take your troubles to Him. Does your world seem to be trembling beneath your feet? Seek protection from the One who cannot be moved. The same God who created the universe will protect you if you ask Him...so ask Him.

The secret of Christian quietness is not indifference, but the knowledge that God is my Father, He loves me, I shall never think of anything He will forget. Then,worry becomes an impossibility.

Oswald Chambers

Dear Lord, forgive me when I worry. Worry reflects a lack of trust in Your ability to meet my every need. Help me to work, Lord, and not to worry. And, keep me mindful, Father, that nothing, absolutely nothing, will happen this day that You and I cannot handle together.

Amen

Worship

But the hour cometh, and now is, when the true worshippers shall worship the Father in spirit and in truth: for the Father seeketh such to worship him.

John 4:23 KJV

Worship the Lord with gladness. Come before him, singing with joy. Acknowledge that the Lord is God! He made us, and we are his. We are his people, the sheep of his pasture....

Psalm 100:2-3 NLT

I was glad when they said unto me, Let us go into the house of the LORD.

Psalm 122:1 KJV

All the earth shall worship thee, and shall sing unto thee; and shall sing to thy name....

Psalm 66:4 KJV

When we worship God, either alone or in the company of fellow believers, we are blessed. When we fail to worship God, for whatever reason, we forfeit the spiritual riches that are rightfully ours. Every day provides opportunities to put God where He belongs: at the center of our lives. Let us worship Him, and only Him, today and always.

The fact that we were created to enjoy God and to worship him forever is etched upon our souls.

Jim Cymbala

In these quiet moments, before this day begins to unfold with all its clamor and distractions, I worship You, Almighty God. May my worship bring You pleasure, and may the time I spend in devotion to You mold me into the person You desire me to be.

Amen